VOLCANOES

SEYMOUR SIMON

Smithsonian | Collins

An Imprint of HarperCollins Publishers

To my sister
Miriam Simon Beyman

PICTURE CREDITS
National Park Service, Hawaii Volcanoes National Park, pages 7, 19, 26; Gary Rosenquist/Earth Images, page 11; Seymour Simon, pages 24, 25, 32; Solarfilma, pages 15, 16, 17; Terraphotographics/BPS, pages 8, 9, 12 (B. J. O'Donnel), 13 (both), 27 (John K. Nakata), 28, 29, 30 (Carl May), 31; U.S. Geological Survey, J. D. Griggs, pages 4, 20, 21, 23.
The name of the Smithsonian, Smithsonian Institution and the sunburst logo
are registered trademarks of the Smithsonian Institution.
Collins is an imprint of HarperCollins Publishers.

Library of Congress Cataloging-in-Publication Data
Simon, Seymour.
Volcanoes / Seymour Simon.
p. cm.
Summary: Explains, in simple terms, the characteristics of volcanoes and describes some famous eruptions and their aftermath.
ISBN-10: 0-06-087716-2 (trade bdg.) — ISBN-13: 978-0-06-087716-3 (trade bdg.)
ISBN-10: 0-06-087717-0 (pbk.) — ISBN-13: 978-0-06-087717-0 (pbk.)
1. Volcanoes—Juvenile literature. [1. Volcanoes.] I. Title.
QE521.3.S56 1988
551.2'1—dc19
87-33316
CIP
AC
1 2 3 4 5 6 7 8 9 10
❖
Revised Edition

Smithsonian Mission Statement

For more than 160 years, the Smithsonian has remained true to its mission, "the increase and diffusion of knowledge." Today the Smithsonian is not only the world's largest provider of museum experiences supported by authoritative scholarship in science, history, and the arts but also an international leader in scientific research and exploration. The Smithsonian offers the world a picture of America, and America a picture of the world.

Natural History Mission Statement

We inspire curiosity, discovery, and learning about nature and culture through outstanding research, collections, exhibitions, and education.

Throughout history, people have told stories about volcanoes. The early Romans believed in Vulcan, their god of fire. They thought that Vulcan worked at a hot forge, striking sparks as he made swords and armor for the other gods. It is from the Roman god Vulcan that we get the word *volcano*.

The early Hawaiians told legends of the wanderings of Pele, their goddess of fire. Pele was chased from her homes by her sister Namaka, goddess of the sea. Pele moved constantly from one Hawaiian island to another. Finally, Pele settled in a mountain called Kilauea, on the Big Island of Hawaii. Even though the islanders tried to please Pele, she burst forth every few years. Kilauea is still an active volcano.

In early times, no one knew how volcanoes formed or why they spouted red-hot molten rock. In modern times, scientists began to study volcanoes. They still don't know all the answers, but they know much about how a volcano works.

Our planet is made up of many layers of rock. The top layers of solid rock are called the crust. Deep beneath the crust is the mantle, where it is so hot that some rock melts. The melted, or molten, rock is called magma.

Volcanoes are formed when magma pushes its way up through the cracks in Earth's crust. This is called a volcanic eruption. When magma pours forth on the surface, it is called lava. In this photograph of an eruption, you can see great fountains of boiling lava forming fiery rivers and lakes. As lava cools, it hardens to form rock that is also called lava.

A volcano is a hill or mountain formed by erupted material that piles up around the vent. Mount Rainier in the state of Washington is an ice-covered volcano that last erupted in the nineteenth century.

Not far from Mount Rainier and another volcano, Mount Adams (top, right), is Mount St. Helens (bottom, left). Native Americans and early settlers in the Northwest had seen Mount St. Helens puff out some ash, steam, and lava in the mid-1800s. Yet for more than a century, the mountain seemed quiet and peaceful.

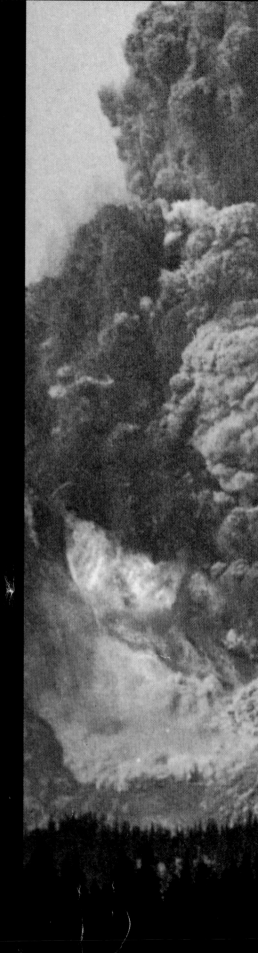

In March 1980, Mount St. Helens awakened from its long sleep. First there were a few small earthquakes that shook the mountain. Then, on March 27, Mount St. Helens began to spout ash and steam. Each day brought further earthquakes, until by mid-May more than ten thousand small earthquakes had been recorded. The mountain began to swell up and crack.

Sunday, May 18, dawned bright and clear. The mountain seemed much the same as it had been for the past month. Suddenly, at 8:32 A.M., Mount St. Helens erupted with incredible force. The energy released in the eruption was equal to ten million tons of dynamite.

The eruption of Mount St. Helens was the most destructive in the history of the United States. Sixty people lost their lives. Measurable ash fell over a huge area of more than 75,000 square miles. Hundreds of houses and cabins were destroyed, leaving many people homeless. Miles of highways, roads, and railways were badly damaged. The force of the eruption was so great that entire forests were blown down like rows of matchsticks.

Compare the way Mount St. Helens looked before and after the eruption. The top of the volcano and a large segment of its north face slid away. In its place is a huge volcanic crater. In 1982, the mountain and the area around it were dedicated as the Mount St. Helens National Volcanic Monument. Visitor centers allow people to view the actively growing lava dome that now partially fills the crater.

Volcanoes don't just happen anyplace. Earth's crust is broken into huge sections like a giant cracked eggshell. The pieces of the crust are called plates. The United States, Canada, Mexico, some of Russia, and the western half of the North Atlantic Ocean are all on the North American plate. Most of the world's volcanoes erupt in places where two plates meet.

Down the middle of the North Atlantic Ocean, two plates are slowly moving apart. Hot magma pushes up between

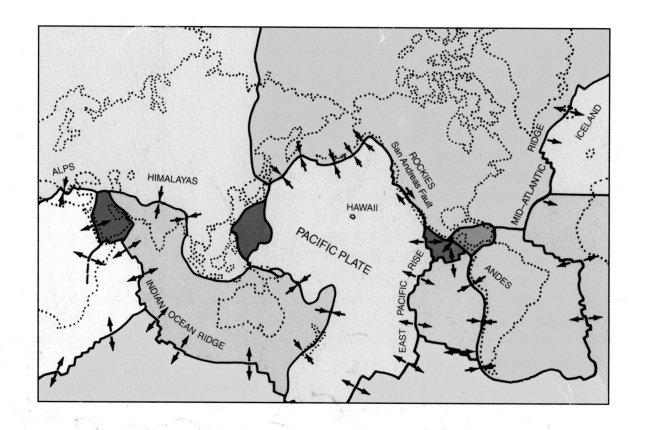

them. A chain of underwater volcanoes runs along the line where the two plates meet. Some of the underwater volcanoes have grown so high that they rise from the ocean floor to above sea level as islands.

Iceland is a volcanic island in the North Atlantic. In 1963, an area of the sea near Iceland began to boil and churn. An undersea volcano was exploding and a new island was being formed. The island was named Surtsey, after the ancient Norse god of fire.

Ten years after the explosion that formed Surtsey, another volcano erupted off the south coast of Iceland on the island of Heimaey. Within six hours of the eruption, more than 5,000 people were taken off the island to safety. After two months, hundreds of buildings had burned down and dozens more had been buried in the advancing lava. Then the volcano stopped erupting. After a year's time, the people of Heimaey came back to reclaim their island with its new 735-foot volcano.

Many volcanoes and earthquakes are located along the margins of the large Pacific plate. Volcanoes and earthquakes are so numerous that these margins are called the "Ring of Fire." But a few volcanoes are not on the edge of a plate. The volcanoes in the Hawaiian Islands are in the middle of the Pacific plate.

These volcanoes have grown, one after another, as the Pacific plate slowly moves to the northwest to form the Hawaiian volcanic chain. Each volcano grew from the deep Pacific seafloor over several million years. Eruption followed eruption, and little by little, thin layers of lava hardened, one atop another. Thousands of eruptions were needed to build mountains high enough to reach from the deep sea bottom and appear as islands.

The largest Hawaiian volcano is Mauna Loa. It is seventy miles long and rises thirty thousand feet from the ocean floor. It is still growing and is one of Hawaii's most active volcanoes.

Hawaiian lava usually gushes out in red-hot fountains a few hundred feet high that feed lava rivers or lakes. Hawaiian volcanoes erupt much less violently than did Surtsey or Mount St. Helens. Only rarely does a Hawaiian volcano throw out rock and high clouds of ash.

Steam clouds billow as a flow of hot lava enters the sea. Hawaii is constantly changing as frequent eruptions of the Mauna Loa and Kilauea volcanoes add hundreds of acres of new land to the Big Island. Old lava flows are quickly weathered by the waves into rocks and black sand.

Hawaiian lava is fluid and flows quickly. In some lava rivers, speeds as high as thirty-five miles per hour have been measured. In an eruption in 1986, a number of houses were threatened by the quick-moving lava. Firefighters sprayed water on the lava to slow down its advance.

When lava cools and hardens, it forms volcanic rocks. The kinds of rocks formed are clues to the kind of eruption. The two main kinds in Hawaii have Hawaiian names. Thick, slow-moving lava called *aa* (AH-ah) hardens into a rough tangle of sharp rocks. Thin, hot, quick-moving lava called *pahoehoe* (pah-HO-ee-ho-ee) forms a smooth, billowy surface.

Earth scientists have divided volcanoes into four groups. Shield volcanoes, such as Mauna Loa and Kilauea, have broad, gentle slopes shaped like an ancient warrior's shield.

Cinder cone volcanoes look like piles of dry sand poured through an opening. They erupt explosively, blowing out red-hot ash and cinders. The ash and cinders build up to form the cone shape. A cinder cone on Pacaya volcano in Guatemala, Central America (above, foreground), has had frequent eruptions.

Most of the volcanoes in the world are composite or stratovolcanoes. Stratovolcanoes are formed by the lava, cinders, and ash from many eruptions. An eruption can be initially explosive, when ash and cinders fall to the ground. Later the eruption becomes less violent and lava slowly flows out, covering the layer of ash and cinders. Further eruptions add more layers of ash and cinders, followed by more layers of lava. Mount Shasta (above) in California and

Mount Hood (below) in Oregon are stratovolcanoes. They are still active even though they have not erupted for many years.

A fourth kind of volcano is called a dome volcano. Dome volcanoes have thick, slow-moving lava that forms a steep-sided dome shape. After an eruption, the volcano may be plugged with hardened lava. The plug prevents the gases from escaping, like a cork in a bottle of soda water. As the pressure builds up, the volcano eventually explodes, as Mount St. Helens did. Lassen Peak in California is a dome volcano that erupted violently in 1915. You can see the huge chunks of volcanic dome rock near the summit.

Around the world there are many very old volcanoes that no longer erupt. Some of these volcanoes are dead and will not erupt again. These are called extinct. Others can be inactive for as long as 50,000 years and then reawaken. These are called dormant. Crater Lake Volcano in Oregon is currently considered dormant, but it is likely to erupt again. Almost seven thousand years ago, its predecessor, Mount Mazama, erupted and covered the ground for thousands of miles around in a blanket of pumice and ash. Toward the end of the eruption, the entire top of the volcano collapsed inward. A huge crater, called a caldera, formed and was later filled with water. Crater Lake reaches a depth of two thousand feet, the deepest lake in North America.

After a volcano erupts, everything is buried under lava or ash. Plants and animals are nowhere to be found. But in a few short months, life renews itself. Plants grow in the cracks between the rocks. Insects and other animals return. Volcanoes do not just destroy. They bring new mountains, new islands, and new soil to the land. Many good things can come from the fiery explosions of volcanoes.